S0-BJL-789

Herbert S. Zim

Alligators and Crocodiles

Newly Revised Edition

illustrated by Jean Zallinger

William Morrow and Company

New York 1978

Printed in the United States of America.
1 2 3 4 5 6 7 8 9 10

Library of Congress Cataloging in Publication Data

Zim, Herbert Spencer (date) Alligators and crocodiles. 1.   Crocodilia — Juvenile literature. I. Zallinger, Jean Day. II. Title.
QL666.C9Z5 1978   598.1'4   78-6615
ISBN 0-688-32170-4 lib. bdg.

Metric measure, now used the world over, is used in this book. Lengths and distances are based on the meter (m); 100 centimeters (cm) make one meter and 1000 meters make one kilometer (km). Weights are in kilograms (kg); 1000 grams (g) make one kilogram (kg), and temperatures are in degrees Celsius (°C).

A meter is just under 40 inches; a kilometer is 0.6 miles. A kilogram equals 2.2 pounds, and 100 degrees Celsius is the same as 212 degrees Fahrenheit.

PROTOSUCHUS, a primitive crocodilian, lived in North America some 175 to 185 million years ago, earlier than most dinosaurs.

Alligators, crocodiles, and their kin, known as the crocodilians, are the last living heirs of the giant reptiles that ruled our planet some 70 to 140 million years ago. These ancient animals roamed the land, plodded through the lush swamps, and swam in the rivers and seas. Of them, the dinosaurs are the best known. But fossils of early crocodilians have been found in even older rocks.

Ancestors to all these creatures were the thecodonts, reptiles that lived some 230 million years ago. A few of the thecodonts looked somewhat like modern alligators and crocodiles. The phytosaurs, a closely related group, were similar in size and shape to the biggest living crocodilians. Some were over 5 meters long. Fossil phytosaur bones have been found in parts of North America and Europe where no crocodilians live today.

DESCENDANTS OF THECODONTS

crocodilians
(living)

bird-hipped dinosaurs
(extinct)

flying reptiles
(extinct)

phytosaurs
(extinct)

typical dinosaur
(extinct)

thecodonts,
ancestral reptiles

DEINOSUCHUS,
a giant, extinct crocodilian,
was 10 to 13 meters long
with a 2-meter skull and large teeth.

By 70 million years ago, nearly all these varied groups of reptiles had died off. The group of modern crocodilians, which appeared late, was one of those that survived. However, through the ages, a large number of crocodilian species became extinct also. *Deinosuchus,* the largest of them, had a skull 2 meters long and a skeleton that stretched for nearly 15 meters. The smallest species was less than a meter long.

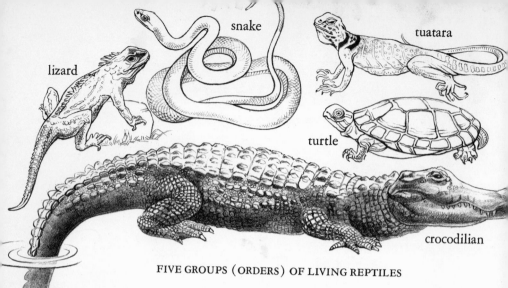

FIVE GROUPS (ORDERS) OF LIVING REPTILES

Today only five small subgroups, or orders, remain of the many reptiles that were important animals for millions of years. The lizards are the most numerous and include about 2,800 species. Then come the snakes, with 2,000 species or so, and the turtles, with only about 220 species. The rare, lizardlike reptile, the tuatara, forms a group all by itself. Finally, the crocodilians compose an order of some 20 or 25 species, depending on which expert has done the counting.

The crocodilian group is made up of two or three families. Some experts combine the alligator family (about 9 species) and the crocodile family (about 15 species) into one. Others separate them into two. In addition, there is the gharial (gavial), a single species that forms a family all by itself. So the crocodilian group is made up almost entirely of alligators and crocodiles. The gators and crocs, as they are often called, are not only the most numerous crocodilians, they are the largest.

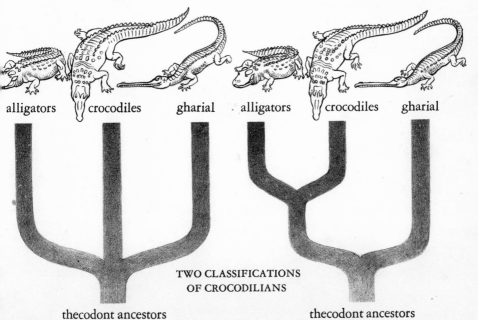

alligators   crocodiles   gharial   alligators   crocodiles   gharial

TWO CLASSIFICATIONS
OF CROCODILIANS

thecodont ancestors   thecodont ancestors

The two or three families of crocodilians differ in minor ways. Some differences are in the details of skull and skeleton, and only an expert would notice them. But even you and I might notice others. For example, crocodiles usually have narrower snouts than alligators. They also have one or two pair of larger teeth in the lower jaw that stick out, overlapping the upper jaw. The gharial has many more teeth, which are smaller, sharper, and better suited for snaring fish.

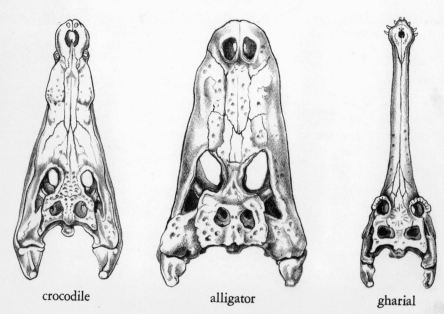

crocodile   alligator   gharial

SKULLS OF THREE CROCODILIANS

The crocodilians and all other reptiles are considered advanced when compared to the fish, frogs, and salamanders that developed before them. Aided by a leathery, scaly skin, reptiles were the first animals to live permanently on land. Lungs enabled them to breathe air directly. An improved heart circulated their blood. Other organs, such as kidneys, were improved also. Reptiles have a well-developed bony skeleton. Most are active, alert animals.

Male reptiles fertilize the eggs of the female while they are still inside her body. After the eggs are fertilized, a hard or tough shell is formed around each. Soon the eggs are laid in a safe nest. Thus, the embryo inside the egg is protected as it develops till it is ready to hatch.

Though advanced in many ways, reptiles do have the disadvantage of being cold-blooded. So are fishes, frogs, salamanders, and many thousands of species of insects and other animals without backbones. All these animals have a body temperature that is about the same as that of their surroundings. They lack any internal means of keeping their body heat constant when the air temperature changes.

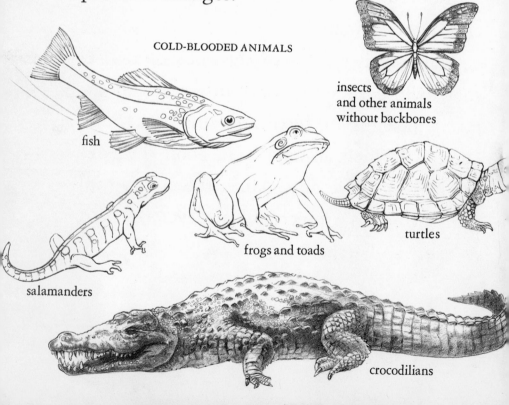

COLD-BLOODED ANIMALS

insects
and other animals
without backbones

fish

salamanders

frogs and toads

turtles

crocodilians

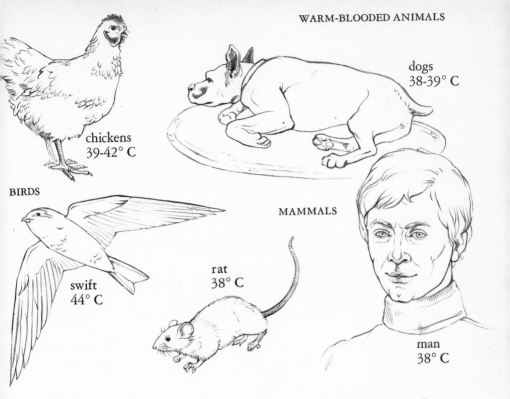

dogs
38-39° C

chickens
39-42° C

BIRDS

MAMMALS

swift
44° C

rat
38° C

man
38° C

Birds and mammals are warm-blooded animals. Their body temperature remains about the same whether the air temperature goes up or down. Their bodies have ways of heating or cooling to keep their temperature constant. Thus, birds and mammals (including yourself) are more active the year round than all reptiles, even the crocodilians.

So crocodilians remain at the mercy of the climate and cannot stand much cold. For this reason, nearly all live in the tropics or in warm temperate areas. Their worldwide distribution lies quite close to the equator.

The two species of alligators are exceptions. They both live in a temperate climate and are limited in their northern range by the

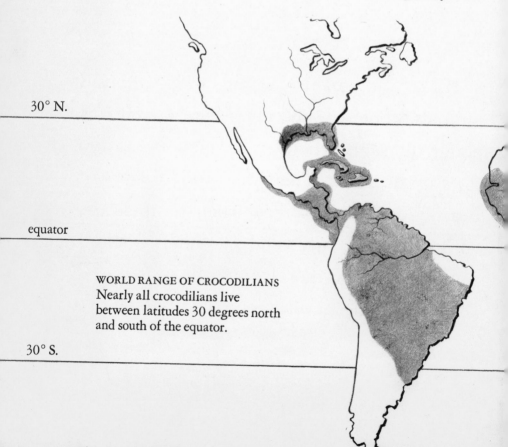

30° N.

equator

WORLD RANGE OF CROCODILIANS
Nearly all crocodilians live
between latitudes 30 degrees north
and south of the equator.

30° S.

cold of winter. But even the crocodiles of the tropics can be endangered by temperature extremes. Too much heat is as bad for them as too much cold. Crocodilians often rest in the shade in summer, not out in the midday sun. If they are still too warm, they return to the water where the temperature is usually lower than on the banks and sandbars.

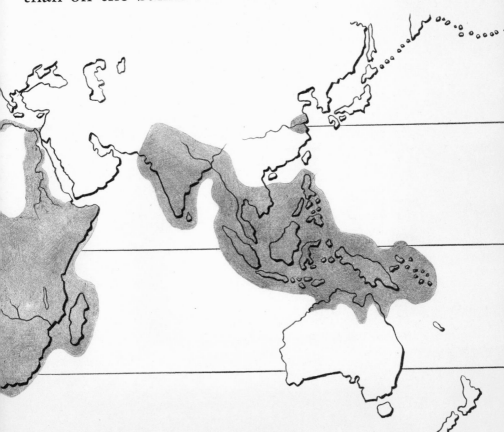

Within these warm areas, crocodilians live in moister habitats than most other reptiles. They never go far from the water, usually staying in swamps, marshes, lagoons, lakes, and rivers. Some like the brackish water at a river's mouth. Others like the salt water of quiet bays and may even go out to sea. They are rarely seen in swift-moving streams but prefer larger, quiet rivers, where they feed in or near the water. There they are safer and more at home.

The long heads of crocodilians show several adaptations for life in water. A flap of skin at the back of the mouth acts as a valve, closing the passage to the throat. The nostrils, near the tip of the snout, connect through a long bony passage to the throat *behind* the flap. So a crocodilian can breathe with only the tip of its snout above the water. Similar valves keep water out of its nostrils and ear openings.

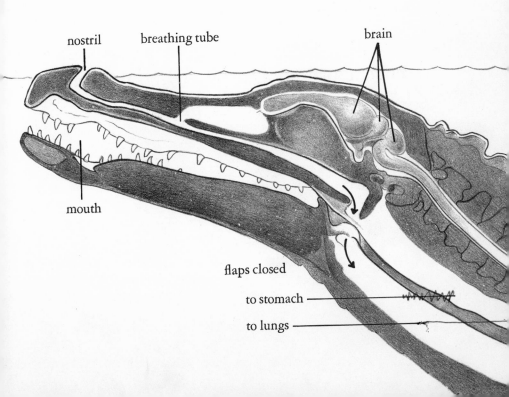

nostril   breathing tube   brain

mouth

flaps closed

to stomach ———

to lungs ———

Hidden in waterweeds, a crocodilian waits motionless till a duck, fish, or other animal comes close. With a sudden plunge and snap the croc grabs its dinner. If there is a struggle, the croc can hold its prey, perhaps a pig, dog, or small deer, underwater to drown it. The croc can breathe without difficulty because of its special air passage.

On land crocs look lazy or sluggish. They lie quietly with their belly in the sand or grass. But if they are aroused or frightened, they rise up on their short legs and can move rapidly. Their front feet have five claws, their back feet only four. All are webbed. With these webbed feet and a broad tail, crocodilians are adept in the water.

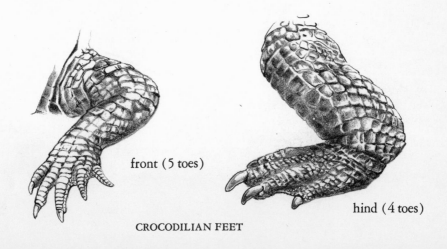

front (5 toes)

hind (4 toes)

CROCODILIAN FEET

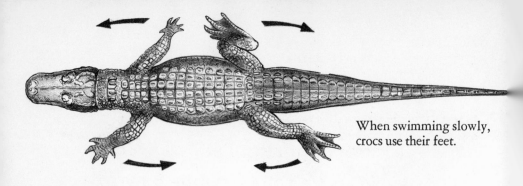

When swimming slowly, crocs use their feet.

A crocodilian uses its feet for slow paddling and to keep its balance in the water. Hind feet are longer and larger than front ones. But if an alligator or crocodile is chasing prey in the water, it uses its tail vigorously and can swim faster than a man can paddle.

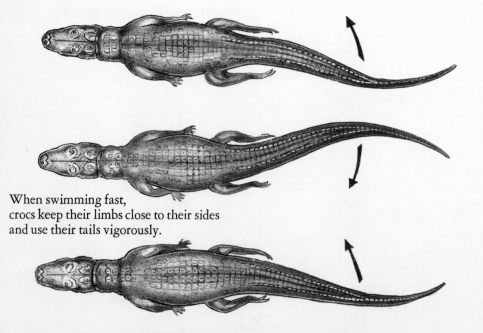

When swimming fast,
crocs keep their limbs close to their sides
and use their tails vigorously.

Crocodilians are considered advanced reptiles because of internal changes that have set them apart from the rest. They have a four-chambered heart (as you do) while other reptiles have only three chambers. A thin muscular sheet, or diaphragm, (also like yours) separates their lungs from the digestive organs. This structure improves the way the crocodilians breathe.

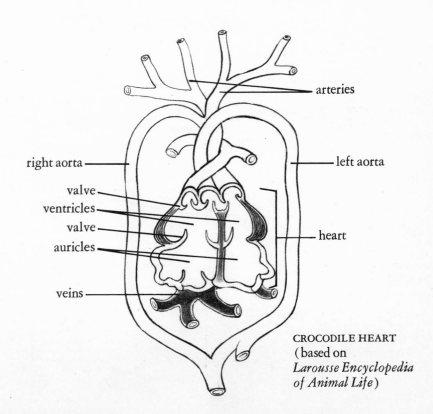

arteries

right aorta

left aorta

valve
ventricles
valve
auricles

heart

veins

CROCODILE HEART
(based on
*Larousse Encyclopedia
of Animal Life*)

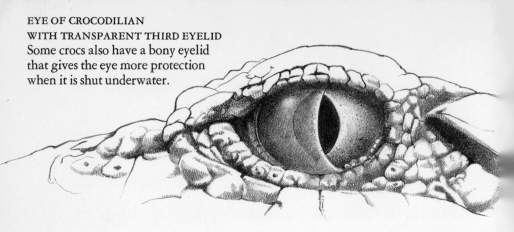

**EYE OF CROCODILIAN
WITH TRANSPARENT THIRD EYELID**
Some crocs also have a bony eyelid
that gives the eye more protection
when it is shut underwater.

The eyes of crocodilians are usually raised, and a transparent cover, or eyelid, can be moved back and forth across them. This cover gives added protection underwater. Each crocodilian has, under its lower jaw, a pair of skin glands that may produce a scent during the mating season. It also has other similar glands about which scientists know very little.

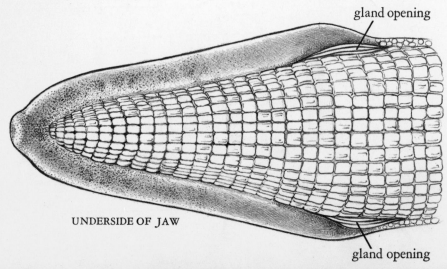

gland opening

UNDERSIDE OF JAW

gland opening

The teeth of crocodilians are developed for grabbing and holding, not for cutting or tearing. You have four types of teeth, each somewhat suited to particular work. Crocodilians have only one type—a conical, pointed tooth—but they total from 20 to 40 or so in each jaw. Teeth in the back of the mouth may be blunter than those in front. A few fish-eating crocodiles and the gharial, which also feeds mainly on fish, have smaller, sharper, and more numerous teeth.

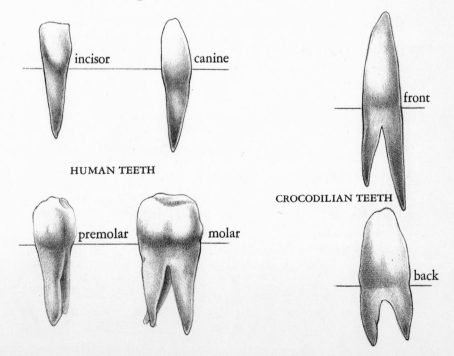

incisor

canine

HUMAN TEETH

premolar

molar

front

CROCODILIAN TEETH

back

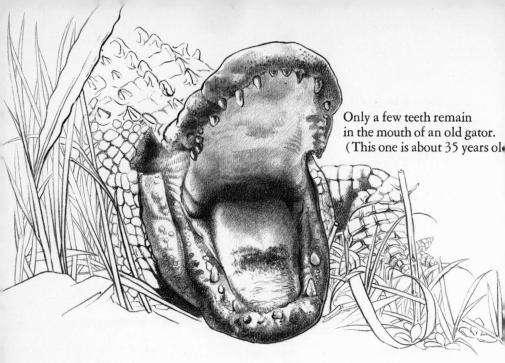

Only a few teeth remain
in the mouth of an old gator.
(This one is about 35 years ol

You grow your teeth twice. The second ones are the final, or adult, set. If any of your adult teeth are lost, they are not replaced. Young crocodilians may replace lost or worn teeth every year or so. New ones grow up from below and fill the empty places. But as crocodilians get older, the replacement stops. Teeth that are lost are not replaced, so a very old croc may be nearly toothless.

The skin of all crocodilians is covered with large scales, which do not overlap like those of snakes. Some of the scales, especially those on the back, have small plates of bone imbedded in them, giving the crocodilian strong armor. Other small bony plates in the skin (as under the throat and between the ribs) add to this protection.

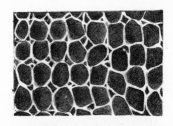

TYPICAL SKIN FROM BELLY OF CROCODILIAN, with scales that do not overlap

SKIN ON BACK OF CROCODILE, with sharp ridges arising from bony plates

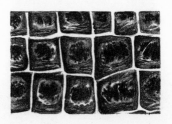

BELLY SKIN OF SOME SPECIES in which flat, bony plates are imbedded

The crocodilian families include by far the largest of the living reptiles. Most lizards, snakes, and turtles—even the larger ones—are smaller than the alligators and crocodiles.

Nearly all lizards are less than a meter long, smaller than the smallest crocodilians. Largest is the Komodo lizard, which may grow 3 meters long and weigh about 80 kilo-

Reptiles killed long ago were reported as quite large, but measurements cannot be confirmed. Those given here are generally accepted today.

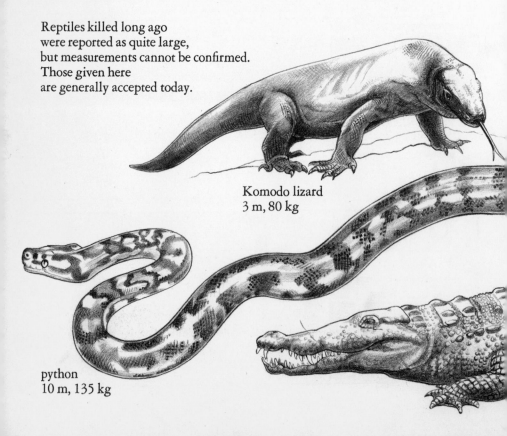

Komodo lizard
3 m, 80 kg

python
10 m, 135 kg

grams. Turtles too are quite small. The leatherback turtle, the largest, is barely 3 meters long, although it may weigh over 500 kilograms. The largest snakes, pythons and anacondas, may be nearly 10 meters long, but rarely weigh over 135 kilograms. The largest crocodilians get to be about 7 meters long and may weigh over 500 kilograms.

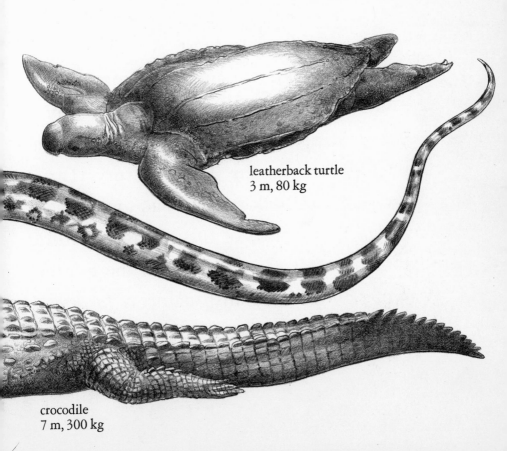

leatherback turtle
3 m, 80 kg

crocodile
7 m, 300 kg

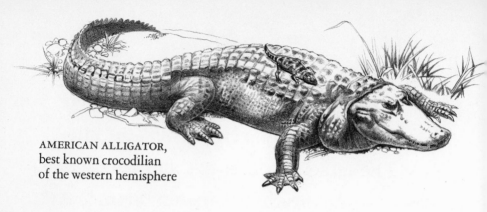

AMERICAN ALLIGATOR,
best known crocodilian
of the western hemisphere

Crocodilians are set off from the other reptiles because of improved structures and functions of their body systems. Even their behavior is somewhat special as a look at the American alligator clearly shows. This alligator is the best known and most common of the nine or so species in the alligator family.

The first Spanish explorers learned of the alligator early in the 16th century. Large skins were sent back to Spain, and with them went fanciful reports of this strange creature. The name itself is no more than the English way of saying its Spanish name, *el lagarto*.

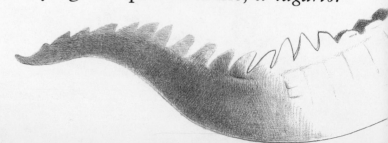

The first alligator stories reported by early explorers and adventurers told of huge man-eating monsters with bullet-proof hides. Because they looked like dragons, some reports had alligators breathing fire and smoke. Their size, feeding habits, and threat to man were all exaggerated. So was their roar, which was said to shake the swamps like thunder during the night.

Even those who first attempted serious studies of alligators had problems in sifting out the facts. Details of the life histories of alligators (and other crocodilians) were not easy to observe at first hand. Scientists often did not have enough experience in the field to know if the reports from hunters and local people were true. Data about courtship, fighting, nest building, care of young, size, age, and strength of crocodilians often included legends and half-truths.

Alligators, when feeding, were reported to knock their prey into the air with their tail and catch it in their mouth as it fell. They were said to rest with mouth open till its entire interior was covered with flies and mosquitoes. Then they would snap their jaws shut and swallow the insects as food.

Though commonly known and widely hunted, the American alligator did not get its official scientific name till the mid-1800's. Studies by trained scientists slowly replaced the legends with even more interesting facts. Bit by bit, details of the gators' life history became known.

In mid-spring alligators begin courting. Mature males and females seek each other out. They tarry together for a few days, the male following the female into shallow water and often stroking her back or sides with his feet.

ALLIGATORS COURTING

Soon after mating, the male and female go their own way. About two months later, the female begins to build her nest. She selects a shady spot, not too far from the water, but high enough so that it will not be flooded. There she makes a pile of leaves, grass, dirt, or sand. The work is slow and may take several days. The debris and dirt may be piled from ½ to 1 meter high and from 1 to 2 meters across. She then hollows out the top of the pile and in the depression lays her eggs.

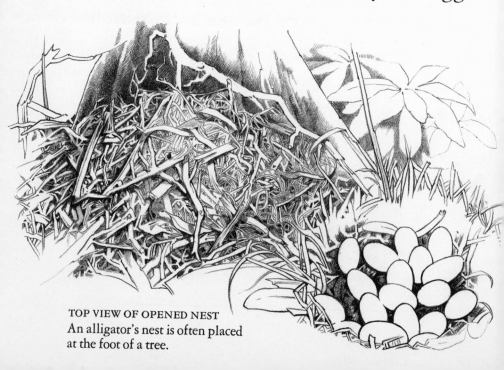

TOP VIEW OF OPENED NEST
An alligator's nest is often placed at the foot of a tree.

FEMALE GATOR GUARDING HER NEST

The female may not begin to lay until a week or so after the nest is finished. Once she starts, she will lay all her eggs in a few hours. From 20 to 70 eggs may go into the nest, but the usual number is more like 30 to 50. The hard-shelled eggs are about 7.5 centimeters long and 5 centimeters in diameter.

Next the female carefully covers her eggs with leaves, sand, or debris. Then she may lie on or near the nest to guard it. If a person or animal comes close, she will rise, snap, and even charge in defense of her nest.

Once laid, the eggs are in a new environment that has its own problems. Skunks, raccoons, and even bears are reported to raid alligator nests and eat the eggs. Greater danger comes from the weather, which may be too hot, too cold, too dry, or too wet. Any of these conditions may keep some or all of the eggs from hatching.

Young alligators break out of their shells aided by an egg tooth at the top of their snout. Later this "tooth" falls off. When the hatchlings wiggle out, they are 20 to 23 centimeters long, dark in color with light, irregular crossbars. They weigh about 60 grams.

BABY ALLIGATOR HATCHING

MARKINGS OF A YOUNG ALLIGATOR

During hatching, the young have been reported to make a grunting noise while still in the egg. This sound brings the female, who helps get them out. Whether she carries them to the water or only guides them, somehow they get there. The distance is not great, and there is no hurry as each hatchling has enough egg yolk in its body to supply food for several days. The young remain in the same shallow area of water for some time.

NEWBORN ALLIGATOR,
full of egg yolk
that is still available for its use

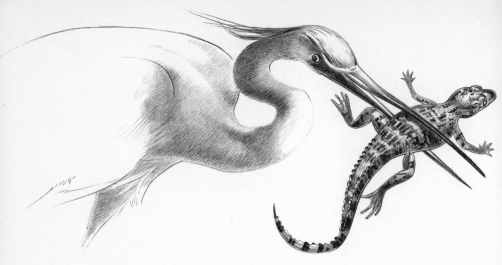

The days and weeks soon after hatching are times of great danger to the young. Vultures, hawks, raccoons, and other animals attack them on land. In the water they fall prey to water snakes, fish, and even large frogs. Herons feed on them, and perhaps large alligators also. For the first year or so, young gators have little protection except to hide.

About half of those that hatch die in the first year and about half of the remainder in the next. Only about 10 percent of all alligators live till they are old enough to breed.

When frightened or threatened, young gators make a high-pitched distress call. Adult alligators seem to recognize it and move toward the sound when they hear it. Adults will even attack whomever or whatever is causing the trouble, as scientists studying alligator families in the field soon discovered.

The first task of young alligators is to find food. Usually there is plenty in the water or on water plants. Shrimps, crawfish, crabs, and similar animals are snatched and eaten. So are any large insects that swim in the water or rest on partly submerged plants. Young alligators also catch small snakes, salamanders, frogs, and whatever fish they can reach.

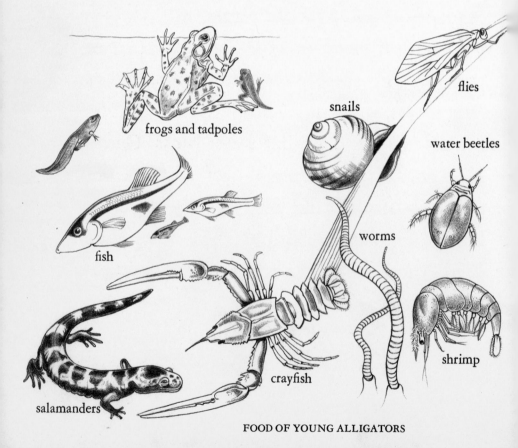

frogs and tadpoles

snails

flies

water beetles

fish

worms

salamanders

crayfish

shrimp

FOOD OF YOUNG ALLIGATORS

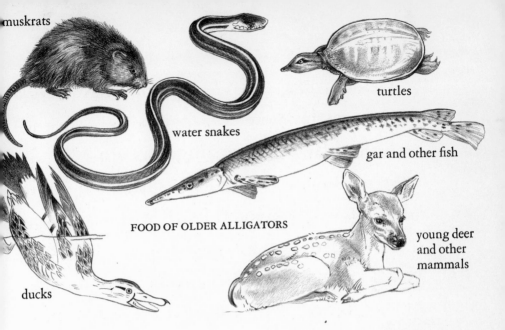

muskrats

water snakes

turtles

gar and other fish

FOOD OF OLDER ALLIGATORS

young deer
and other
mammals

ducks

Older alligators take larger fish such as gar, sunfish, and perch. They eat turtles, crushing the shells with their strong teeth. Water rats, muskrats, and nutria are caught. So are ducks and similar water birds. Gators seize dogs, pigs, and small deer as they come down to drink. They feed mainly on back-boned animals, including those they find dead. There are only a few records of people killed by alligators.

If they survive a year, gators may weigh 250 grams or more and may be 60 centimeters long. By the time alligators are 125 centimeters long, they can be considered adult. They grow rapidly and in 10 years or so may measure 3 meters long and weigh 135 kilograms or more. Anything larger is rare. The record size for gators is close to 6 meters in

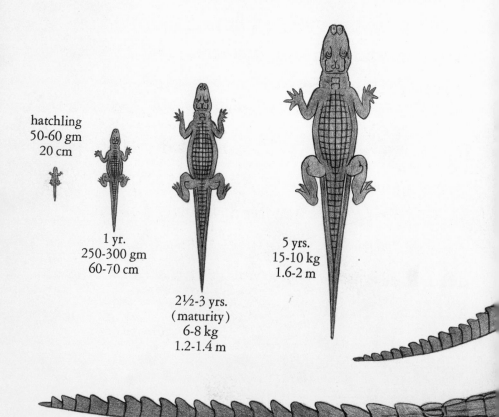

hatchling
50-60 gm
20 cm

1 yr.
250-300 gm
60-70 cm

2½-3 yrs.
(maturity)
6-8 kg
1.2-1.4 m

5 yrs.
15-10 kg
1.6-2 m

length and 300 kilograms or more in weight. There seems no clear difference in size between young males and females. Once fully grown, female gators may be somewhat smaller than males.

10 yrs.
100-150 kg
3-3.5 m

record
300+ kg
6 or more m

Alligators get their prey by stealth and concealment. They lie so quietly in the water that they are mistaken for water-soaked logs. As long as water is plentiful, the alligator has no problem. But in some swamps and marshes the water supply dwindles with the dry season. Gators search for natural holes of deeper water and may enlarge them to make gator holes. If the water level drops enough, these gator holes may be the only wet places left. By then fish and other water animals have moved into them. Hence, the gators have a food supply and a safe place to live.

If the gator lives in a large river or lake, it may find a deepwater bank and dig itself a den. This den may be a shallow shelf or a fairly deep tunnel. Gators have even used small caves with an underwater entrance.

As the weather gets colder in winter, the alligator becomes less and less active. It remains in its den or hole, eating very little or not at all. On a warm day it may come out and bask in the sun, but it may also remain hidden till spring has clearly come.

GATOR DEN

Alligators do not form lasting family groups or live together in colonies. But when conditions are good and food is plentiful, large numbers can be seen in the same area. Such populations run from hatchlings to old adults. Young gators do tend to remain near the female for a year and sometimes longer. However, all those seen in the same gator hole are not necessarily in one family. When alligators were plentiful, several females would often nest in the same area, but this behavior is no longer common.

EVERGLADES GATOR HOLE

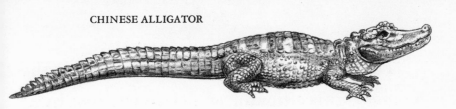

The other species commonly called alligator comes from China. In the 3rd century, the Chinese wrote of a water dragon. Marco Polo, the Italian traveler, recorded it in the 13th century, telling how it was hunted for its meat and skin. This "dragon" was first seen by European scientists about a hundred years ago. They soon learned that China, as well as America, had its own alligator.

The Chinese alligator has a more turned-up nose and other features different from the American's. It is less than 2 meters long, with a heavier body and a shorter tail. Little is known of its food, but it may feed more on river turtles than on other animals since it has heavier teeth.

The Yangtze River in central China is the home of this alligator, which in the past lived in a much larger part of the river valley. Because the winters are cold, the Chinese alligator burrows a meter or more into the riverbank and stays there through the cold months. With the spring rains and warmth, it becomes active and appears again.

The Chinese alligator has been hunted till only a few remain. During the 1960's and 70's limited sightings of it were reported. Experts are worried that this badly threatened species may soon be extinct.

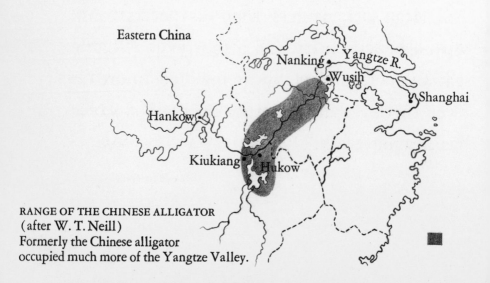

RANGE OF THE CHINESE ALLIGATOR
(after W. T. Neill)
Formerly the Chinese alligator
occupied much more of the Yangtze Valley.

Also grouped in the alligator family are several species of caiman — alligatorlike crocodilians that live in Central and South America. They are common in the Amazon Valley and along the eastern coast. Most caimans differ from gators in having a bony ridge over each eye with a connecting bony bridge between.

The black caiman seems to feed more on the edge of lakes and ponds than in the water. It is reported to lunge after its prey, which is often a large water rodent known as the capybara. This fairly large crocodilian has been reported to be up to 5 meters long.

Naming the different species of crocodilians is a problem for scientists because of conflicting opinions on the importance of differences they find. Sometimes these differences are distinctive enough so that each form is considered a separate species.

In the case of the spectacled caiman, which is the most common of the caimans in South America, four distinct forms are recorded. However, the differences are minor and the forms have enough in common so that most experts consider each a race, or subspecies.

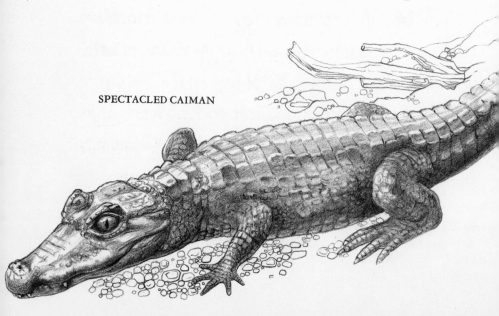

SPECTACLED CAIMAN

Other interesting species in the alligator family are two smooth-fronted caimans. They are so called because both lack the bony ridges around the eyes that other caimans have. These species are more heavily armored than the others and have bony plates in nearly every part of their skin. They even have a bone in each eyelid.

Both of these caimans live in northern South America. The smaller one (less than 2 meters long) is also called the dwarf caiman. It prefers streams while the larger one (over 2 meters long) chooses more quiet waters.

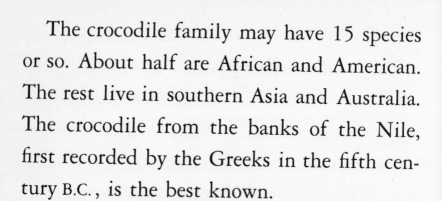

SEBEK, THE EGYPTIAN CROCODILE GOD

MUMMY OF A YOUNG NILE CROCODILE WRAPPED IN LINEN

The crocodile family may have 15 species or so. About half are African and American. The rest live in southern Asia and Australia. The crocodile from the banks of the Nile, first recorded by the Greeks in the fifth century B.C., is the best known.

Even earlier, the Egyptians worshipped a crocodile god, and mummies of Nile crocodiles have been found in tombs at Tebtynis on the Nile. Sacred crocs are still venerated in Africa. Some live in temple pools, attended by a priest. Many myths and legends about crocodilians can be traced back to the Nile crocodile.

The Nile croc is found throughout Africa (except in the northern and southern deserts) and on the nearby islands too. It lives in large rivers and coastal swamps. Long ago it was found along the southern and eastern shores of the Mediterranean Sea.

After centuries of being hunted for its much-prized skin, the Nile crocodile no longer occupies the Nile Delta. It is only common in out-of-the-way and protected areas, as in some of Africa's famous game parks. This and similar species are now raised on "farms" in Thailand, Papua, and elsewhere.

CROC FARM IN THAILAND

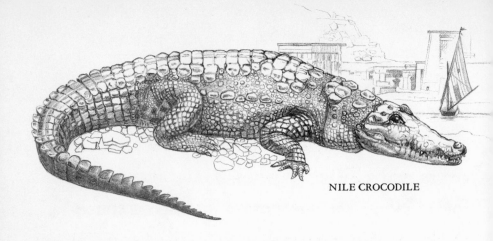

NILE CROCODILE

Nile crocodiles court and mate in shallow water. Some months later, as the dry season gets under way, the female lays 20 to 80 eggs in a shallow pit dug on a nearby beach or bank. She covers them with dirt and debris and then remains on guard close by. She stays without eating for twelve weeks or so, while the eggs incubate. Thus, she keeps the nest from being dug up by baboons, mongooses, monitor lizards, or warthogs searching for the eggs. She uses the same nesting area year after year.

As is said of the American alligator, the female is reported to hear the cry of the hatching young and to dig open the nest to help them escape. Then she carries the hatchlings to the water in her mouth. The male may help also. Her young stay with her for quite some time before they drift away on their own. No other modern reptile provides so much care for its offspring.

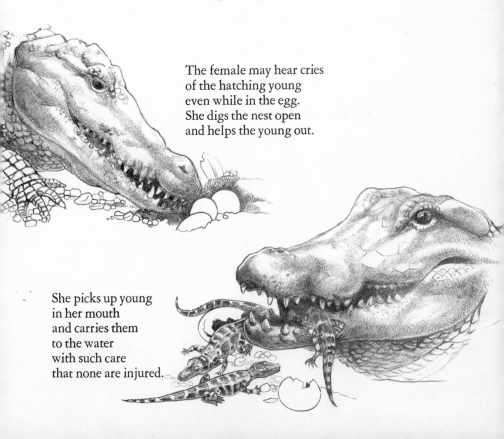

The female may hear cries of the hatching young even while in the egg. She digs the nest open and helps the young out.

She picks up young in her mouth and carries them to the water with such care that none are injured.

SALTWATER CROCODILE

Almost as well known is the saltwater crocodile, a species of the East Indies that ranges from India to northern Australia. This croc goes far out to sea, covering hundreds of miles between islands, yet it nests and raises young only where fresher water is available for them. It has less bony armor in its skin than other species, which perhaps improves its ability as a long-distance swimmer. The adults also occupy salt marshes and larger rivers.

This rapidly growing species may add 50 centimeters a year in length when young and

about half that as it gets older. The largest
reported was over 6 meters long, but 3
meters is more common. The saltwater crocodile may feed on deer and cattle. It also at-
tacks men, even those fishing in small boats.
It may have killed or injured more people
than all the other crocodilians put together.
This ugly reputation seems to be deserved for
the one species only, but it gives all the
crocodilians a bad name.

Crocodiles have long been known in Africa, Australia, and South Asia, but they were not identified in Florida till 1822. The same species was discovered earlier in Mexico and Central and South America. It is rightly called the American crocodile.

Both alligators and crocodiles live in southern Florida, where alligators are by far the most common. American crocs are thinner and more agile than gators. Their mark-

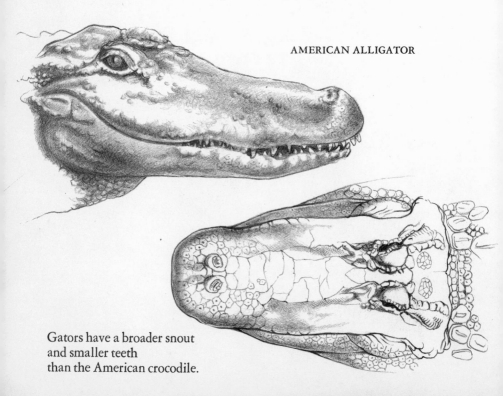

AMERICAN ALLIGATOR

Gators have a broader snout
and smaller teeth
than the American crocodile.

ings differ. Young crocs are gray with black crossbars; young gators are black with yellow crossbars. Heads and snouts of crocs are narrower; eyes stand out and ear openings are more visible. The tooth arrangement is typical of crocodiles; the fourth tooth on each side of the lower jaw overlaps the upper jaw. Crocodiles are found in coastal areas and salt marshes, alligators in freshwater lakes, rivers, and swamps.

AMERICAN CROCODILE

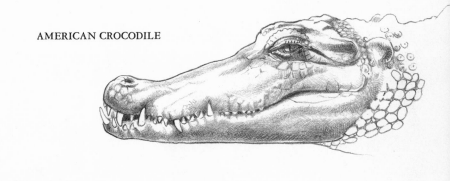

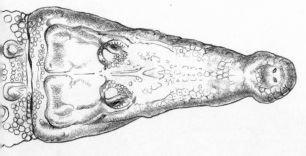

The croc has a narrow snout. Large teeth from lower jaw overlap the upper jaw.

Of the western-hemisphere crocodiles, the American has the largest range. Before it was hunted for its hide, it was the most common. But by 1978, airplane surveys showed that only about 200 crocodiles remained in Florida from a population that was estimated at over 2000. All the large ones are gone, including the largest ever measured—4.8 meters. Nowadays American crocodiles are rarely more than half that size.

Not until 1976 did the United States put the American crocodile on its endangered species list. Even with this late protection, the American crocodile may survive only in inaccessible areas.

AMERICAN CROCODILE

young croc (enlarged)

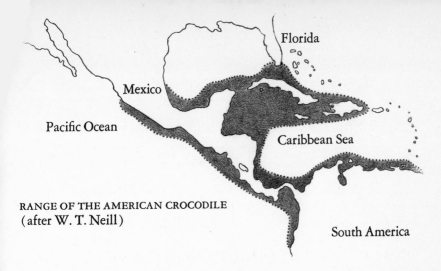

RANGE OF THE AMERICAN CROCODILE
(after W. T. Neill)

Three other New World crocodiles have more limited ranges than the American. The Orinoco crocodile (up to about 4 meters) is most like the American in appearance and habits. Its long, narrow snout rises at the tip.

Farther north, in the Yucatán peninsula of Mexico, is Morelet's crocodile, named after a biological explorer. This one, with a fairly broad snout, lives in ponds, lakes, and streams, where it grows some 2 meters long. Years of hunting have made it rare, and it is seldom seen.

CUBAN CROCODILE

The last and most specialized of New World crocodiles is the Cuban species, found only in a limited area on this island. The American crocodile lives in Cuba also, but each species prefers a special environment. The Cuban croc lives in freshwater swamps and marshes, the American in large rivers and along the coast.

The Cuban croc is more armored with heavy bony plates than other American crocodiles. Its teeth are large, and a bony ridge extends behind each eye. It has the reputation of a fierce fighter.

Oddly, there are pygmy species in the family that includes the largest reptiles. Two kinds of pygmy crocodiles live in the warm, wet rain forests of Central Africa. The Congo dwarf crocodile is not much over 1 meter long. This rare crocodile seems to be a primitive one.

The other is the West African dwarf crocodile. It can be recognized by the strongly tipped-up nose. This species gets to be some 2 meters long, making it something more than a dwarf. It lives on the coast, where it is also seen in salt or brackish water.

CONGO CROCODILE

TOMISTOMA,
a specialized fish-eating crocodile

Somewhat different from other crocodiles is the false gavial, better known as the tomistoma. A narrow-snouted croc of Malay and Indonesia, it lives in rivers, grows up to be 5 meters long, feeds on fish, and lays the largest eggs of any crocodilian.

Even more interesting is the true gavial, now called the gharial, its correct name. It is the only survivor of a family that goes back at least 50 million years. Found mainly in the river valleys of India (especially in the Ganges), it may grow almost 7 meters long. Some males have an overgrowth, or hump, at the tip of their long, narrow snout.

The gharial, with its small, sharp teeth, is a fish eater, though it may also eat small birds and mammals. Gharials are reported as timid and becoming more and more scarce.

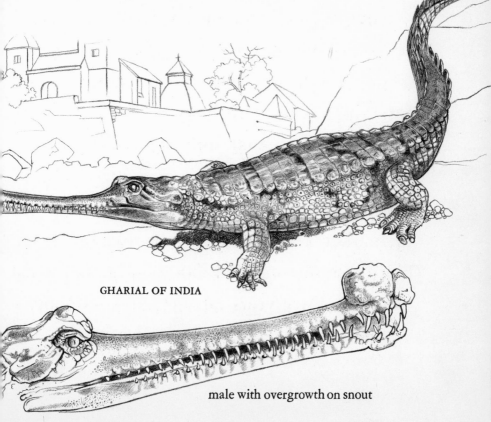

GHARIAL OF INDIA

male with overgrowth on snout

Experts are not sure why the great reptiles of ancient times became extinct. But they do know why their large living relatives, the crocodilians, are headed for the same fate. People are their doom. Crocodilians are not especially dangerous nor are they needed as food. They are hunted because their skins are prized for belts, bags, and fancy shoes.

Men and women of fashion in America and Europe came close to wiping out beavers (for hats and furs), leopards and monkeys (for furs), herons and other water birds (for hats and hair ornaments), and now they may do the same to the crocodilians. Some two million skins of crocodilians have been shipped to market every year. In the early 1900's, Florida alone shipped 200,000 gator skins annually. Fifty years later there were none.

The few giant reptiles still living are now in danger. A number of species are on the official list as endangered or threatened. But steps are being taken to stop hunting of crocodilians and limit the sale of their skins. Several countries have stopped the practice entirely. Experts have urged that marshlands and estuaries, where many crocodilians live, be protected too.

The tide now seems to be turning. American alligators are on the increase. More protected areas are set aside. Perhaps there is hope that these living fossils, strange and interesting, will always be around to remind us of the ancient days of the giant reptiles.

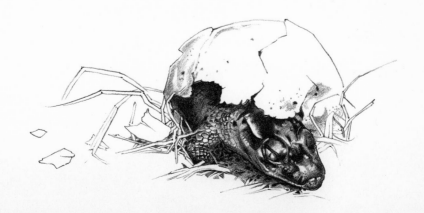

INDEX

indicates illustration